DELICIOUSLY LIGHT: LOW FAT RECIP.

First edition. March 19, 2024.

Copyright © 2024 Caveley Maureen Anne.

ISBN: 979-8224398126

Written by Caveley Maureen Anne.

Table of Contents

Deliciously Light: Low Fat Recipes For Healthy Living

Stir-fried tofu with broccoli and bell peppers

Ingredients:

- 1 block tofu (14 oz)
- 1 head broccoli
- 2 bell peppers
- 2 tbsp soy sauce
- 1 tbsp sesame oil
- 1 tsp garlic powder
- 1 tsp ginger powder

Equipment:

1. Wok
2. Spatula
3. Cutting board
4. Knife
5. Bowl

Methods:

Step 1: Heat oil in a large skillet or wok over medium heat.

Step 2: Add cubed tofu and stir fry until lightly browned, about 5 minutes.

Step 3: Remove tofu from the skillet and set aside.

Step 4: In the same skillet, add chopped broccoli and bell peppers.

Step 5: Stir fry the vegetables until they are tender-crisp, about 5 minutes.

Step 6: Add the tofu back into the skillet.

Step 7: Pour in your favorite stir-fry sauce and toss everything together.

Step 8: Cook for an additional 2-3 minutes until everything is heated through.

Step 9: Serve hot over rice or noodles. Enjoy!

Helpful Tips:

1. Press tofu before cooking to remove excess water and help it get crispier.
2. Use a non-stick pan or wok for stir-frying to prevent sticking.
3. Start by sautéing garlic, ginger, and onions for extra flavor.
4. Add tofu and cook until golden brown before adding vegetables.

5. Cook broccoli and bell peppers until slightly tender but still crisp.

6. Season with soy sauce, sesame oil, and a pinch of sugar for a balanced flavor.

7. Garnish with sesame seeds or green onions for added texture and freshness.

Roasted salmon with dill and lemon

Ingredients:

- 4 salmon fillets
- 4 tbsp olive oil
- 1 lemon, sliced
- 4 tbsp fresh dill
- Salt and pepper to taste

Equipment:

1. Baking sheet
2. Oven
3. Frying pan
4. Mixing bowl
5. Knife

Methods:

Step 1: Preheat the oven to 375°F and line a baking sheet with parchment paper.

Step 2: Place a salmon fillet on the prepared baking sheet.

Step 3: Drizzle the salmon with olive oil and sprinkle with salt and pepper.

Step 4: Thinly slice a lemon and lay the slices on top of the salmon.

Step 5: Chop fresh dill and sprinkle over the salmon.

Step 6: Bake in the preheated oven for 15-20 minutes, or until the salmon is cooked through and flakes easily with a fork.

Step 7: Serve the roasted salmon with additional dill and lemon slices, if desired. Enjoy!

Helpful Tips:

1. Preheat the oven to 400°F and line a baking sheet with foil.

2. Place the salmon on the baking sheet and season with salt, pepper, and olive oil.

3. Sprinkle chopped fresh dill and slices of lemon over the salmon.

4. Roast in the oven for 12-15 minutes, or until the salmon is opaque and flakes easily with a fork.

5. Serve with additional dill and lemon wedges for garnish.

6. For added flavor, try adding minced garlic or red pepper flakes to the seasoning.

7. Enjoy your delicious and healthy roasted salmon with dill and lemon!

Turkey and vegetable stir fry

Ingredients:

- 1 lb turkey breast, sliced
- 2 cups mixed vegetables
- 1/4 cup soy sauce
- 2 cloves garlic, minced
- 1 tbsp olive oil

Equipment:

1. Wok
2. Cutting board
3. Knife
4. Wooden spoon
5. Tongs

Methods:

Step 1: Heat oil in a large skillet or wok over medium-high heat.

Step 2: Add cubed turkey breast and cook until browned on all sides.

Step 3: Remove turkey from skillet and set aside.

Step 4: In the same skillet, add sliced bell peppers, broccoli florets, and sliced carrots.

Step 5: Cook vegetables until slightly tender, about 5 minutes.

Step 6: Add minced garlic and ginger to the skillet and cook for another minute.

Step 7: Return the cooked turkey to the skillet.

Step 8: In a small bowl, mix together soy sauce, hoisin sauce, and a splash of sesame oil.

Step 9: Pour sauce over the turkey and vegetables and stir to combine.

Step 10: Serve the turkey and vegetable stir fry over rice or noodles. Enjoy!

Helpful Tips:

1. Start by preparing all your ingredients beforehand to make the cooking process smoother.

2. Choose a lean cut of turkey meat and slice it thinly for quicker cooking.

3. Heat your wok or skillet over high heat before adding oil for a crispy stir-fry.

4. Cook the turkey first until it's almost cooked through before adding vegetables to avoid overcooking them.

5. Season with soy sauce, garlic, ginger, and your favorite stir-fry sauce for a flavorful dish.

6. Serve over steamed rice or noodles for a complete meal. Enjoy!

Grilled shrimp and avocado salad

Ingredients:

- 1 lb large shrimp
- 2 avocados
- 1 red onion
- 1 yellow bell pepper
- 1/4 cup olive oil
- 1/4 cup lime juice
- Salt and pepper to taste

Equipment:

1. Knife
2. Cutting board
3. Mixing bowl
4. Grill pan
5. Tongs

Methods:

Step 1: Preheat the grill to medium-high heat.

Step 2: In a small bowl, combine olive oil, garlic, lemon juice, salt, and pepper to make a marinade.

Step 3: Peel and devein the shrimp, then toss them in the marinade.

Step 4: Place the shrimp on skewers and grill for 2-3 minutes per side, or until cooked through.

Step 5: Cut the avocados in half, remove the pits, and scoop out the flesh.

Step 6: In a large bowl, combine the grilled shrimp, avocado, mixed greens, cherry tomatoes, and dressing.

Step 7: Toss to coat and serve immediately. Enjoy your grilled shrimp and avocado salad!

Helpful Tips:

1. Start by marinating the shrimp in a mixture of garlic, lemon juice, and olive oil for at least 30 minutes.

2. Use large shrimp for grilling to prevent them from overcooking quickly.

3. Preheat the grill to medium-high heat and cook the shrimp for 2-3 minutes per side until charred and pink.

4. Toss together diced avocado, cherry tomatoes, red onion, and arugula in a large bowl.

5. Drizzle with a lemon vinaigrette dressing and season with salt and pepper to taste.

6. Top the salad with the grilled shrimp and serve immediately for a delicious and healthy meal.

Greek yogurt parfait with fresh fruit

Ingredients:

- 2 cups Greek yogurt
- 2 cups fresh fruit (berries, kiwi, mango)
- 1/2 cup granola
- 1/4 cup honey

Equipment:

1. Mixing bowl
2. Whisk
3. Spoon
4. Parfait glass
5. Knife
6. Cutting board

Methods:

Step 1: Gather your ingredients - Greek yogurt, fresh fruits (such as berries, bananas, and mangoes), granola, and honey.

Step 2: In a glass or bowl, layer the Greek yogurt at the bottom.

Step 3: Top the yogurt with a layer of mixed fresh fruits.

Step 4: Sprinkle granola on top of the fruit layer.

Step 5: Drizzle honey over the granola layer.

Step 6: Repeat the layering process until the glass or bowl is full.

Step 7: Serve immediately and enjoy your delicious Greek yogurt parfait with fresh fruit!

Helpful Tips:

1. Start by layering the bottom of your glass with your choice of granola for added crunch.

2. Add a generous spoonful of Greek yogurt on top of the granola layer for a creamy and protein-packed base.

3. Choose a variety of fresh fruits like berries, sliced bananas, or diced mango to add a burst of sweetness and vitamins.

4. Repeat the layers until you reach the top of your glass, finishing with a dollop of yogurt and a sprinkle of granola.

5. Drizzle with honey or agave for added sweetness, if desired. Enjoy your nutritious and delicious Greek yogurt parfait!

Baked sweet potato with salsa

Ingredients:

- 4 sweet potatoes
- 1 red onion
- 2 tomatoes
- 1 lime
- Cilantro
- Olive oil
- Salt, pepper

Equipment:

1. Baking sheet
2. Knife
3. Vegetable peeler
4. Mixing bowl
5. Cutting board

Methods:

Step 1: Preheat the oven to 400°F.

Step 2: Wash and dry the sweet potatoes.

Step 3: Pierce the sweet potatoes all over with a fork.

Step 4: Place the sweet potatoes on a baking sheet and bake for 45-60 minutes, or until tender.

Step 5: While the sweet potatoes are baking, prepare the salsa by chopping tomatoes, onions, and cilantro and mixing them together in a bowl.

Step 6: Once the sweet potatoes are cooked, slice them open and fluff the insides with a fork.

Step 7: Top each sweet potato with salsa and serve hot. Enjoy your delicious baked sweet potato with salsa!

Helpful Tips:

1. Preheat the oven to 400°F.
2. Wash and scrub the sweet potatoes thoroughly.
3. Pierce the sweet potatoes with a fork a few times.

4. Rub olive oil over the sweet potatoes and sprinkle with salt and pepper.

5. Place the sweet potatoes on a baking sheet and bake for about 45-60 minutes until tender.

6. While the sweet potatoes are baking, prepare the salsa by mixing diced tomatoes, onions, jalapenos, cilantro, lime juice, salt, and pepper in a bowl.

7. Once the sweet potatoes are done, let them cool slightly before topping with salsa.

8. Serve hot and enjoy your delicious baked sweet potato with salsa!

Black bean soup with cilantro

Ingredients:

- 2 cans black beans
- 1 onion, chopped
- 2 cloves garlic, minced
- 4 cups chicken broth
- 1/2 cup chopped cilantro
- Salt and pepper to taste

Equipment:

1. Pot
2. Ladle
3. Cutting board
4. Knife
5. Blender

Methods:

Step 1: In a large pot, sauté chopped onions and garlic in olive oil until translucent.

Step 2: Add in diced carrots, celery, and bell peppers and cook until slightly softened.

Step 3: Pour in vegetable broth and bring to a boil.

Step 4: Stir in canned black beans, cumin, chili powder, and salt and pepper to taste.

Step 5: Simmer for 20 minutes to allow flavors to meld together.

Step 6: Remove from heat and use an immersion blender to blend soup until smooth.

Step 7: Serve hot, garnished with fresh cilantro leaves. Enjoy your delicious black bean soup with cilantro!

Helpful Tips:

1. Rinse and soak the black beans overnight to reduce cooking time and improve digestibility.

2. Use vegetable broth instead of water for added flavor.

3. Sauté generous amounts of onions, garlic, and bell peppers for a savory base.

4. Add cumin, chili powder, and smoked paprika for depth of flavor.

5. Blend half of the soup for a creamy texture, then mix it back in.

6. Garnish with fresh cilantro and a squeeze of lime before serving.

7. Serve with a dollop of sour cream or Greek yogurt for added creaminess.

Baked tilapia with green beans

Ingredients:

- 4 tilapia fillets
- 2 cups green beans
- 2 tbsp olive oil
- 1 lemon, sliced
- Salt and pepper to taste

Equipment:

1. Baking dish
2. Frying pan
3. Tongs
4. Spatula
5. Mixing bowl
6. Knife

Methods:

Step 1: Preheat the oven to 375°F.

Step 2: Season the tilapia fillets with salt, pepper, and your favorite herbs.

Step 3: Place the seasoned tilapia fillets in a baking dish.

Step 4: Drizzle the fillets with olive oil and a squeeze of lemon juice.

Step 5: Bake the tilapia in the oven for 15-20 minutes, or until the fish is cooked through.

Step 6: While the tilapia is baking, steam the green beans until they are tender-crisp.

Step 7: Serve the baked tilapia with the steamed green beans on the side.

Step 8: Enjoy your delicious and healthy meal!

Helpful Tips:

1. Preheat your oven to 400°F and line a baking sheet with parchment paper.

2. Season your tilapia fillets with salt, pepper, and any desired herbs or spices.

3. Place the seasoned tilapia on the baking sheet and arrange fresh green beans around the fillets.

4. Drizzle olive oil over the fish and vegetables, then sprinkle with lemon juice.

5. Bake in the preheated oven for 15-20 minutes, or until the fish flakes easily with a fork.

6. Serve hot and enjoy your delicious and nutritious meal!

Vegetable stir fry with tofu

Ingredients:

- 1 block of firm tofu (14 oz)
- 2 cups mixed vegetables
- 1/4 cup soy sauce
- 2 cloves of garlic
- 1 tbsp sesame oil
- 1 tsp ginger
- Rice or noodles (optional)

Equipment:

1. Wok
2. Spatula
3. Tongs
4. Knife
5. Cutting board

Methods:

Step 1: Heat oil in a large skillet or wok over medium-high heat.

Step 2: Add diced tofu into the hot skillet and cook until golden brown on all sides.

Step 3: Remove tofu from skillet and set aside.

Step 4: Add sliced vegetables (such as bell peppers, broccoli, and carrots) to the skillet and stir fry until tender-crisp.

Step 5: Mix in tofu and add a sauce made of soy sauce, garlic, ginger, and a pinch of sugar.

Step 6: Cook for a few more minutes until everything is heated through.

Step 7: Serve the vegetable stir fry with tofu over rice or noodles. Enjoy!

Helpful Tips:

1. Press tofu between paper towels with a heavy object to remove excess water.

2. Cut tofu into cubes and marinate in soy sauce, garlic, and ginger for added flavor.

3. Use a mix of colorful veggies like bell peppers, broccoli, and snap peas for a visually appealing stir fry.

4. Cook tofu in a hot skillet with oil until golden brown on all sides before adding veggies.

5. Add a sauce made from soy sauce, sesame oil, and cornstarch to coat the veggies and tofu.

6. Serve stir fry over cooked rice or noodles for a balanced meal.

Roasted chicken breast with Brussels sprouts

Ingredients:

- 4 chicken breasts
- 1 lb Brussels sprouts
- 1 tbsp olive oil
- Salt and pepper to taste

Equipment:

1. Knife
2. Cutting board
3. Baking sheet
4. Roasting pan
5. Tongs

Methods:

Step 1: Preheat the oven to 400°F.

Step 2: Season the chicken breast with salt, pepper, and any other desired seasonings.

Step 3: Place the chicken breast on a baking sheet lined with parchment paper.

Step 4: In a separate bowl, toss Brussels sprouts with olive oil, salt, pepper, and garlic powder.

Step 5: Spread the seasoned Brussels sprouts around the chicken breast on the baking sheet.

Step 6: Roast in the oven for 25-30 minutes, or until the chicken is cooked through and the Brussels sprouts are crispy.

Step 7: Let the chicken rest for a few minutes before serving. Enjoy your roasted chicken breast with Brussels sprouts!

Helpful Tips:

1. Preheat your oven to 425°F.

2. Season the chicken breast with salt, pepper, and your preferred herbs or spices.

3. Trim the Brussels sprouts and toss them in olive oil, salt, and pepper.

4. Place the chicken breast on a baking sheet and surround with the Brussels sprouts.

5. Roast in the preheated oven for about 25-30 minutes, or until the chicken is cooked through and the Brussels sprouts are tender.

6. For extra flavor, add lemon slices or garlic cloves to the pan while roasting.

7. Let the chicken rest for a few minutes before slicing and serving. Enjoy!

Shrimp and vegetable stir fry

Ingredients:
- 1 lb shrimp
- 2 cups mixed vegetables
- 1/3 cup soy sauce
- 2 tbsp olive oil
- 1 tsp garlic
- 1 tsp ginger

Equipment:
1. Wok
2. Wooden spoon
3. Cooking pan
4. Chef's knife
5. Cutting board

Methods:
Step 1: Peel and devein 1 pound of shrimp.

Step 2: Heat a large skillet over medium-high heat and add 1 tablespoon of oil.

Step 3: Add the shrimp to the skillet and cook for 2-3 minutes on each side, until pink and cooked through. Remove from skillet and set aside.

Step 4: In the same skillet, add 1 thinly sliced bell pepper, 1 cup of sliced carrots, and 1 cup of broccoli florets.

Step 5: Cook for 3-4 minutes, until vegetables are tender-crisp.

Step 6: Add the shrimp back to the skillet and stir in 1/4 cup of soy sauce and 1 tablespoon of minced garlic.

Step 7: Cook for another 2-3 minutes, until everything is heated through.

Step 8: Serve hot over rice or noodles. Enjoy your shrimp and vegetable stir fry!

Helpful Tips:
1. Preheat your wok or skillet before adding any ingredients to ensure a quick and even cook.

2. Use high heat and cook the shrimp in batches to avoid overcrowding the pan.

3. Marinate the shrimp in a mixture of soy sauce, garlic, and ginger for added flavor.

4. Add vegetables like bell peppers, broccoli, and snap peas for a colorful and nutritious stir fry.

5. Stir constantly to prevent sticking and ensure even cooking.

6. Finish with a splash of lime juice and a sprinkle of sesame seeds for a burst of freshness.

7. Serve over steamed rice or noodles for a complete meal.

Grilled turkey burger with lettuce wrap

Ingredients:
- 1 lb ground turkey
- 1/4 cup diced red onion
- 1/4 cup chopped parsley
- 1 tsp garlic powder
- 1 tsp salt
- 1 tsp pepper
- 4 large lettuce leaves

Equipment:
1. Grill
2. Spatula
3. Knife
4. Cutting board
5. Mixing bowl
6. Plate

Methods:
Step 1: Preheat the grill to medium-high heat.

Step 2: Season ground turkey with salt, pepper, and desired seasonings.

Step 3: Form turkey into burger patties and place on grill.

Step 4: Grill burgers for about 5-6 minutes per side, or until internal temperature reaches 165°F.

Step 5: Wash lettuce leaves and pat dry to use as wraps.

Step 6: Once burgers are cooked through, remove from grill and let rest for a few minutes.

Step 7: Place burger patty on lettuce leaf and add desired toppings.

Step 8: Wrap lettuce around burger and enjoy your delicious and healthy grilled turkey burger!

Helpful Tips:
1. Season ground turkey patties with your favorite spices like garlic powder, onion powder, salt, and pepper.

2. Preheat the grill to medium-high heat and brush with oil to prevent sticking.

3. Grill the turkey burgers for about 5-6 minutes per side, or until they reach an internal temperature of 165°F.

4. Serve the turkey burgers on a lettuce wrap instead of a bun for a low-carb option.

5. Top with your favorite toppings like sliced tomato, onion, avocado, and a dollop of Greek yogurt or hummus for added flavor. Enjoy!

Cucumber and tomato salad with balsamic dressing

Ingredients:
- 2 cucumbers
- 4 tomatoes
- 2 tbsp balsamic vinegar
- 2 tbsp olive oil
- Salt and pepper to taste

Equipment:
1. Knife
2. Cutting board
3. Mixing bowl
4. Whisk
5. Salad tongs

Methods:
Step 1: Wash and chop 2 cucumbers and 4 tomatoes into bite-sized pieces.

Step 2: In a small bowl, mix 2 tablespoons of balsamic vinegar, 1 tablespoon of olive oil, and a pinch of salt and pepper.

Step 3: Toss the chopped cucumbers and tomatoes in the balsamic dressing until evenly coated.

Step 4: Let the salad marinate in the refrigerator for at least 30 minutes.

Step 5: When ready to serve, sprinkle with chopped fresh basil or parsley for garnish.

Step 6: Enjoy your refreshing cucumber and tomato salad with balsamic dressing as a side dish or light meal.

Helpful Tips:
1. Start by thinly slicing the cucumbers and tomatoes for a consistent texture.

2. Use a mix of red and yellow cherry tomatoes for added color and flavor.

3. To make the balsamic dressing, combine balsamic vinegar, olive oil, honey, and a pinch of salt and pepper in a small bowl.

4. Toss the sliced cucumbers and tomatoes in the balsamic dressing until well coated.

5. Let the salad marinate in the fridge for at least 30 minutes before serving to enhance the flavors.

6. Sprinkle with fresh herbs like basil or parsley before serving for an extra burst of freshness.

Baked chicken thighs with rosemary and garlic

Ingredients:
- 4 bone-in, skin-on chicken thighs
- 2 tablespoons olive oil
- 4 cloves garlic, minced
- 1 tablespoon fresh rosemary, chopped

Equipment:
1. Mixing bowl
2. Baking sheet
3. Tongs
4. Measuring spoons
5. Knife
6. Oven

Methods:
Step 1: Preheat your oven to 375°F.

Step 2: In a small bowl, mix together chopped rosemary, minced garlic, olive oil, salt, and pepper.

Step 3: Pat dry the chicken thighs and place them in a baking dish.

Step 4: Brush the chicken thighs with the rosemary and garlic mixture, making sure to coat them evenly.

Step 5: Bake in the preheated oven for about 45-50 minutes, or until the chicken is cooked through and golden brown.

Step 6: Serve hot and enjoy your delicious baked chicken thighs with rosemary and garlic.

Helpful Tips:
1. Preheat oven to 400 degrees Fahrenheit.
2. Rub chicken thighs with olive oil and season with salt and pepper.
3. Place chicken thighs in a baking dish.
4. Sprinkle minced garlic and fresh rosemary over the chicken thighs.
5. Cover the baking dish with foil and bake for 25 minutes.

6. Remove foil and bake for an additional 10-15 minutes until chicken is cooked through and golden brown.

7. Serve hot with your favorite side dishes.

8. For added flavor, you can squeeze fresh lemon juice over the chicken before serving.

9. Enjoy your delicious baked chicken thighs with rosemary and garlic!

Stir fried bok choy with tofu

Ingredients:

- 1 block tofu, cubed
- 4 heads bok choy, chopped
- 2 cloves garlic, minced
- 2 tbsp soy sauce
- 1 tbsp sesame oil
- Salt and pepper to taste

Equipment:

1. Wok or Skillet
2. Tongs or Spatula
3. Knife
4. Cutting Board
5. Bowl for Marinating Tofu
6. Serving Plate

Methods:

Step 1: Heat oil in a large skillet or wok over medium-high heat.

Step 2: Add cubed tofu and stir fry until golden brown, about 5 minutes.

Step 3: Remove tofu from skillet and set aside.

Step 4: Add chopped bok choy and garlic to the skillet.

Step 5: Stir fry bok choy until tender-crisp, about 3-4 minutes.

Step 6: Add soy sauce, sesame oil, and a pinch of red pepper flakes to the skillet.

Step 7: Return tofu to the skillet and toss everything together.

Step 8: Cook for an additional 2 minutes.

Step 9: Remove from heat and serve hot. Enjoy your stir fried bok choy with tofu!

Helpful Tips:

1. Start by preparing all your ingredients: bok choy, tofu, garlic, soy sauce, sesame oil, and any other desired seasonings.

2. Press tofu to remove excess moisture before cutting into cubes to ensure a crispy texture when stir-frying.

3. Heat a wok or large skillet over high heat and add oil, then tofu cubes to brown on all sides.

4. Add minced garlic and sliced bok choy, stirring frequently until bok choy is wilted but still slightly crisp.

5. Stir in soy sauce and sesame oil just before serving for a flavorful finish. Serve hot over rice or noodles. Enjoy!

Eggplant parmesan with marinara sauce

Ingredients:

- 2 large eggplants
- 2 cups marinara sauce
- 1 cup grated parmesan cheese
- 1 cup breadcrumbs

Equipment:

1. Skillet
2. Wooden spoon
3. Baking dish
4. Chef's knife
5. Grater

Methods:

Step 1: Preheat the oven to 375°F.

Step 2: Slice the eggplant into 1/4 inch thick rounds.

Step 3: Salt the eggplant slices and let them sit for 30 minutes to remove excess moisture.

Step 4: Rinse the eggplant slices and pat them dry.

Step 5: Dip the eggplant slices in beaten eggs, then coat with breadcrumbs.

Step 6: Heat a skillet with olive oil and cook the eggplant slices until golden brown on both sides.

Step 7: In a baking dish, layer marinara sauce, eggplant slices, and shredded mozzarella and parmesan cheese.

Step 8: Repeat the layers and bake for 25 minutes until the cheese is bubbly and golden brown. Enjoy your delicious eggplant parmesan with marinara sauce!

Helpful Tips:

1. Start by slicing the eggplant into 1/4 inch rounds and sprinkle with salt to help draw out excess moisture.

2. After about 30 minutes, pat the eggplant dry with paper towels and dip each slice into beaten egg before coating with a mixture of breadcrumbs and parmesan cheese.

3. Fry the coated eggplant slices in hot oil until golden brown on both sides.

4. Layer the fried eggplant in a baking dish with marinara sauce and shredded mozzarella cheese.

5. Bake in a preheated oven at 350°F for about 25-30 minutes until bubbly and golden brown on top.

6. Serve hot and enjoy!

Roasted vegetable medley with balsamic glaze

Ingredients:

- 2 medium zucchinis, sliced
- 2 large red bell peppers, sliced
- 1 red onion, sliced
- 1/4 cup balsamic vinegar
- 2 tbsp olive oil
- Salt and pepper to taste

Equipment:

1. Baking sheet
2. Mixing bowl
3. Chef's knife
4. Cutting board
5. Saute pan
6. Wooden spoon

Methods:

Step 1: Preheat oven to 400°F.

Step 2: Cut vegetables such as bell peppers, zucchini, squash, and red onions into bite-sized pieces.

Step 3: Toss vegetables with olive oil, salt, and pepper in a large bowl.

Step 4: Spread vegetables evenly on a baking sheet lined with parchment paper.

Step 5: Roast in the oven for 25-30 minutes, or until vegetables are tender and slightly browned.

Step 6: In a small saucepan, heat balsamic vinegar and honey over medium heat until it thickens into a glaze.

Step 7: Drizzle balsamic glaze over roasted vegetables before serving. Enjoy your roasted vegetable medley with balsamic glaze!

Helpful Tips:

1. Use a variety of colorful vegetables such as bell peppers, zucchini, cherry tomatoes, and red onions for a visually appealing dish.

2. Cut the vegetables into similar sizes to ensure even cooking.

3. Toss the vegetables with olive oil, salt, and pepper before roasting in a preheated oven at 400°F.

4. Halfway through cooking, drizzle balsamic glaze over the vegetables for added flavor.

5. Don't overcrowd the baking sheet to allow for proper caramelization.

6. Garnish with fresh herbs like basil or parsley before serving.

7. Serve as a side dish or atop a bed of quinoa or couscous for a wholesome meal.

Lemon herb grilled chicken with asparagus

Ingredients:

- 4 chicken breasts
- 1/4 cup lemon juice
- 2 tbsp olive oil
- 2 cloves garlic, minced
- 1 tsp thyme
- 1 tsp rosemary
- 1/2 tsp salt
- 1/4 tsp pepper
- 1 lb asparagus

Equipment:

1. Grill pan
2. Tongs
3. Grill brush
4. Basting brush
5. Knife
6. Cutting board

Methods:

Step 1: Marinate chicken breasts in a mixture of lemon juice, olive oil, minced garlic, and chopped herbs (such as rosemary, thyme, and parsley).

Step 2: Preheat grill to medium-high heat.

Step 3: Grill marinated chicken breasts for 6-8 minutes on each side, or until fully cooked.

Step 4: Toss asparagus with olive oil, salt, and pepper.

Step 5: Grill asparagus for 4-5 minutes, or until slightly charred and tender.

Step 6: Serve grilled chicken with asparagus on the side.

Step 7: Enjoy your delicious lemon herb grilled chicken with asparagus!

Helpful Tips:

1. Marinate the chicken in a mixture of lemon juice, garlic, herbs, salt, and pepper for at least 30 minutes before grilling.

2. Preheat your grill to medium-high heat and oil the grates to prevent sticking.

3. Grill the chicken for about 6-8 minutes per side, or until it reaches an internal temperature of 165°F.

4. Toss the asparagus with olive oil, salt, and pepper before grilling in a grill basket or foil packet.

5. Grill the asparagus for 5-7 minutes, turning occasionally, until tender.

6. Serve the grilled chicken and asparagus together with extra lemon wedges for squeezing. Enjoy your delicious and healthy meal!

Baked halibut with cherry tomatoes

Ingredients:

- 4 halibut fillets
- 2 cups cherry tomatoes
- 4 cloves garlic
- 1/4 cup olive oil
- Salt and pepper to taste

Equipment:

1. Baking dish
2. Frying pan
3. Spatula
4. Knife
5. Cutting board

Methods:

Step 1: Preheat the oven to 400°F.

Step 2: Place the halibut fillets in a baking dish.

Step 3: Drizzle the halibut with olive oil and season with salt and pepper.

Step 4: Add cherry tomatoes around the fish.

Step 5: Drizzle cherry tomatoes with olive oil and sprinkle with salt and pepper.

Step 6: Add garlic cloves and fresh herbs like thyme or dill.

Step 7: Bake in the preheated oven for 20-25 minutes, or until the fish is cooked through and flaky.

Step 8: Serve hot and enjoy your baked halibut with cherry tomatoes!

Helpful Tips:

1. Preheat the oven to 400°F.

2. Season the halibut fillets with salt, pepper, and any herbs or spices you like.

3. Place the cherry tomatoes in a baking dish and drizzle with olive oil.

4. Nestle the seasoned halibut fillets amongst the tomatoes.

5. Squeeze some lemon juice over the fish and tomatoes.

6. Bake in the oven for about 15-20 minutes, or until the fish is opaque and flakes easily.

7. Garnish with fresh herbs before serving.

8. Serve with a side of rice or vegetables for a complete meal. Enjoy!

Chicken and spinach salad with light dressing

Ingredients:
- 2 grilled chicken breasts
- 4 cups baby spinach
- 1/2 cup cherry tomatoes
- 1/4 cup sliced almonds
- Light vinaigrette dressing

Equipment:
1. Mixing bowl
2. Whisk
3. Salad tongs
4. Salad spinner
5. Cutting board
6. Knife

Methods:
Step 1: Begin by marinating the chicken breasts in olive oil, lemon juice, and a mix of your favorite herbs and spices.

Step 2: Grill the marinated chicken until fully cooked and then allow it to cool before slicing into thin strips.

Step 3: In a large bowl, combine fresh spinach leaves, cherry tomatoes, sliced cucumbers, and diced red onion.

Step 4: Top the salad with the sliced grilled chicken strips.

Step 5: In a separate bowl, whisk together olive oil, balsamic vinegar, honey, and Dijon mustard to create a light dressing.

Step 6: Drizzle the dressing over the salad and toss until well combined.

Step 7: Serve the chicken and spinach salad with light dressing immediately and enjoy!

Helpful Tips:
1. Start by marinating the chicken in a mixture of lemon juice, olive oil, garlic, and herbs for extra flavor.

2. Grill or bake the chicken until it reaches an internal temperature of 165°F to ensure it is fully cooked.

3. While the chicken is cooking, wash and dry the spinach thoroughly to remove any dirt or grit.

4. Toss the spinach with cherry tomatoes, sliced cucumbers, and any other desired vegetables.

5. For the light dressing, mix together olive oil, balsamic vinegar, Dijon mustard, and a pinch of salt and pepper.

6. Top the salad with sliced chicken breast and drizzle with the dressing just before serving. Enjoy your healthy and delicious meal!

Broccoli and tofu stir fry

Ingredients:

- 1 lb firm tofu
- 1 head broccoli
- 2 tbsp soy sauce
- 2 cloves garlic

Equipment:

1. Wok
2. Wooden spoon
3. Chef's knife
4. Cutting board
5. Tongs

Methods:

Step 1: Cut the tofu into cubes and boil the broccoli until slightly tender.

Step 2: Heat oil in a pan and add the tofu cubes, cook until golden brown.

Step 3: Add chopped garlic and ginger to the pan and cook for a minute.

Step 4: Add the boiled broccoli to the pan and stir fry for a few minutes.

Step 5: In a separate bowl, mix soy sauce, rice vinegar, and sesame oil.

Step 6: Pour the sauce over the broccoli and tofu mixture and stir well.

Step 7: Cook for a few more minutes until heated through.

Step 8: Serve hot over rice or noodles.

Helpful Tips:

1. Make sure to drain and press the tofu beforehand to remove excess moisture for better texture.

2. Heat oil in a large skillet or wok before adding the broccoli and tofu to ensure proper cooking and browning.

3. Use a flavorful sauce like soy sauce, garlic, ginger, and sesame oil to enhance the taste of the dish.

4. Stir frequently to avoid sticking and ensure even cooking of the ingredients.

5. Consider adding other veggies or protein sources like bell peppers, mushrooms, or chicken for variety and added nutrients.

Cauliflower rice with mixed vegetables

Ingredients:
- 1 head of cauliflower
- 1 cup mixed vegetables
- 1/2 onion, chopped
- 2 cloves garlic, minced
- 1 tbsp olive oil
- Salt and pepper to taste

Equipment:
1. Saucepan
2. Knife
3. Cutting board
4. Skillet
5. Wooden spoon

Methods:
Step 1: Start by chopping a head of cauliflower into small florets.

Step 2: Place the cauliflower florets into a food processor and pulse until it resembles rice grains.

Step 3: Heat a large skillet over medium heat and add a tablespoon of olive oil.

Step 4: Add the cauliflower rice to the skillet and cook for 5-7 minutes, stirring occasionally.

Step 5: In the meantime, chop up your favorite vegetables such as bell peppers, carrots, and peas.

Step 6: Add the vegetables to the skillet with the cauliflower rice and cook for an additional 5 minutes.

Step 7: Season with salt, pepper, and any other desired seasonings.

Step 8: Serve hot and enjoy your delicious cauliflower rice with mixed vegetables!

Helpful Tips:
1. Start by heating some oil in a pan over medium heat.

2. Add finely chopped onions and garlic for flavor.

3. Stir in the cauliflower rice and cook for a few minutes until slightly softened.

4. Add in your choice of mixed vegetables such as bell peppers, carrots, and peas.

5. Season with salt, pepper, and your favorite herbs or spices.

6. Cook until the vegetables are tender yet still have a slight crunch.

7. Serve hot as a side dish or main course.

8. For added flavor, consider adding soy sauce or a splash of lemon juice before serving.

Grilled shrimp skewers with pineapple

Ingredients:
- 1 lb shrimp
- 1 pineapple
- 1/4 cup olive oil
- 2 tbsp soy sauce
- 1 tbsp lemon juice
- Salt and pepper to taste

Equipment:
1. Grill skewers
2. Tongs
3. Cutting board
4. Knife
5. Mixing bowl

Methods:
Step 1: Preheat the grill to medium-high heat.

Step 2: Soak wooden skewers in water for at least 30 minutes to prevent burning.

Step 3: Thread shrimp and pineapple chunks onto the skewers alternately.

Step 4: Brush skewers with oil and season with salt, pepper, and any desired seasonings like garlic powder or paprika.

Step 5: Place skewers on the grill and cook for 2-3 minutes per side, until shrimp is pink and opaque.

Step 6: Remove skewers from the grill and let cool for a few minutes before serving.

Step 7: Enjoy your delicious grilled shrimp skewers with pineapple!

Helpful Tips:
1. Soak wooden skewers in water for at least 30 minutes to prevent them from burning on the grill.

2. Marinate the shrimp in a mixture of olive oil, garlic, lemon juice, and your favorite seasonings for at least 30 minutes before cooking.

3. Alternate threading the shrimp and pineapple chunks onto the skewers for a delicious combination of flavors.

4. Preheat the grill to medium-high heat and cook the skewers for 2-3 minutes per side, or until the shrimp is pink and opaque.

5. Serve the skewers with a side of rice or a fresh salad for a complete and satisfying meal. Enjoy!

Baked eggplant with tomato sauce and mozzarella

Ingredients:

- 1 large eggplant
- 1 cup of tomato sauce
- 1 cup of shredded mozzarella cheese
- Salt and pepper to taste

Equipment:

1. Baking tray
2. Knife
3. Cutting board
4. Saucepan
5. Grater

Methods:

Step 1: Preheat the oven to 400°F (200°C).

Step 2: Slice the eggplant into rounds and place them in a colander. Sprinkle with salt and let sit for 20 minutes to draw out excess moisture.

Step 3: Rinse the eggplant under cold water and pat dry with paper towels.

Step 4: In a baking dish, spread a layer of tomato sauce on the bottom.

Step 5: Arrange the eggplant slices on top of the tomato sauce.

Step 6: Top the eggplant with more tomato sauce and a layer of mozzarella cheese.

Step 7: Bake in the preheated oven for 25-30 minutes, or until the cheese is bubbly and golden brown.

Step 8: Serve hot and enjoy!

Helpful Tips:

1. Preheat your oven to 375°F (190°C).

2. Slice the eggplant into rounds and sprinkle with salt to draw out any bitterness.

3. Rinse the salt off the eggplant and pat dry before brushing with olive oil.

4. Roast the eggplant slices in the oven until they are soft and starting to brown.

5. In a separate pan, simmer your favorite tomato sauce on the stovetop.

6. Layer the roasted eggplant slices with the tomato sauce and shredded mozzarella in a baking dish.

7. Bake in the oven for 15-20 minutes or until the cheese is melted and bubbly.

8. Serve hot and enjoy your delicious baked eggplant dish!

Turkey lettuce wraps with hoisin sauce

Ingredients:
- 1 lb ground turkey
- 1/3 cup hoisin sauce
- 1 head iceberg lettuce
- 1/4 cup chopped green onions

Equipment:
1. Skillet
2. Wooden spoon
3. Knife
4. Cutting board
5. Wok
6. Tongs

Methods:
Step 1: Heat a large skillet over medium-high heat

Step 2: Add ground turkey to the skillet and cook until browned

Step 3: Stir in minced garlic, ginger, and sliced water chestnuts

Step 4: Add hoisin sauce, soy sauce, and rice vinegar to the skillet

Step 5: Cook for an additional 2-3 minutes, until heated through

Step 6: Separate lettuce leaves and rinse under cold water

Step 7: Spoon the turkey mixture onto each lettuce leaf

Step 8: Top with chopped green onions and crushed peanuts

Step 9: Roll up the lettuce leaves and serve as a healthy and delicious appetizer or meal.

Helpful Tips:
1. Start by marinating thin slices of turkey breast in a mixture of hoisin sauce, soy sauce, and garlic for maximum flavor.

2. Use iceberg or butter lettuce leaves as a sturdy base for your wraps.

3. Don't overcook the turkey slices to keep them juicy and tender.

4. Add some crunch with diced water chestnuts or sliced almonds for texture.

5. Top with sliced green onions, cilantro, and a squeeze of fresh lime juice for a burst of freshness.

6. Serve with extra hoisin sauce on the side for dipping. Enjoy your flavorful and healthy turkey lettuce wraps!

Grilled white fish with mango salsa

Ingredients:

- 4 white fish fillets
- 1 ripe mango
- 1 red onion
- 1 red bell pepper
- Cilantro
- Lime juice
- Olive oil
- Salt
- Pepper

Equipment:

1. Mixing bowl
2. Chef's knife
3. Cutting board
4. Grill pan
5. Tongs

Methods:

Step 1: Preheat your grill to medium heat.

Step 2: Season the white fish fillets with salt, pepper, and a squeeze of lemon juice.

Step 3: Place the fish fillets on the grill and cook for about 4-5 minutes on each side, or until the fish is cooked through and flaky.

Step 4: In a bowl, combine diced mango, red onion, jalapeno, cilantro, lime juice, and a pinch of salt to make the salsa.

Step 5: Remove the fish from the grill and top with the mango salsa.

Step 6: Serve the grilled white fish with mango salsa hot and enjoy!

Helpful Tips:

1. Start by marinating the white fish in a mixture of lemon juice, olive oil, salt, and pepper for 30 minutes to add flavor.

2. Preheat your grill to medium-high heat and make sure it's well-oiled to prevent sticking.

3. Grill the fish for about 4-5 minutes on each side, or until it's cooked through and opaque.

4. For the mango salsa, combine diced mango, red onion, jalapeno, cilantro, lime juice, and a pinch of salt in a bowl.

5. Serve the grilled fish topped with the mango salsa for a refreshing and flavorful dish. Enjoy!

Egg white and vegetable scramble

Ingredients:

- 8 egg whites
- 1 bell pepper
- 1 onion
- 1 zucchini
- 1 tomato
- Salt and pepper to taste

Equipment:

1. Skillet
2. Spatula
3. Whisk
4. Mixing bowl
5. Grater

Methods:

Step 1: Heat a non-stick skillet over medium heat.

Step 2: In a bowl, whisk together 4 egg whites and a splash of water.

Step 3: Add diced vegetables of your choice (such as bell peppers, onions, and spinach) to the skillet and cook until they are softened.

Step 4: Pour the egg white mixture over the vegetables in the skillet.

Step 5: Cook, stirring occasionally, until the eggs are fully cooked and scrambled.

Step 6: Season with salt, pepper, and any herbs or spices you like.

Step 7: Serve hot and enjoy your healthy and delicious egg white and vegetable scramble.

Helpful Tips:

1. Start by whisking together the egg whites with a splash of milk or water to make them fluffier.

2. Sauté your favorite vegetables in a non-stick pan with a small amount of olive oil or cooking spray.

3. Once the veggies are tender, pour in the egg whites and cook until they are fully set.

4. Season with salt, pepper, and any other herbs or spices you like.

5. Serve hot with a side of whole grain toast or fresh fruit for a balanced meal.

6. Leftovers can be stored in the fridge and reheated for a quick breakfast or snack.

Baked chicken drumsticks with honey mustard glaze

Ingredients:

- 8 chicken drumsticks
- 1/4 cup honey
- 2 tbsp whole grain mustard
- 1 tbsp olive oil
- Salt and pepper to taste

Equipment:

1. Baking tray
2. Cooking brush
3. Tongs
4. Aluminum foil
5. Oven mitts

Methods:

Step 1: Preheat the oven to 400°F.

Step 2: In a small bowl, mix together 1/4 cup honey, 2 tablespoons Dijon mustard, 1 tablespoon olive oil, and salt and pepper to taste.

Step 3: Place 6 chicken drumsticks on a baking sheet lined with foil.

Step 4: Brush the honey mustard glaze over the chicken drumsticks, making sure to coat them evenly.

Step 5: Bake the chicken drumsticks for 35-40 minutes, or until they are cooked through and golden brown.

Step 6: Remove from the oven and let rest for a few minutes before serving.

Step 7: Enjoy your delicious baked chicken drumsticks with honey mustard glaze!

Helpful Tips:

1. Preheat your oven to 375°F and line a baking sheet with parchment paper.

2. Season your chicken drumsticks with salt, pepper, and any other desired spices.

3. In a small bowl, mix together honey, mustard, and a splash of olive oil for the glaze.

4. Brush the honey mustard glaze onto the drumsticks, making sure they are evenly coated.

5. Bake the drumsticks for 35-40 minutes, or until they are cooked through and the glaze is caramelized.

6. Serve hot and enjoy the delicious sweet and tangy flavor of the honey mustard glaze.

Grilled portobello mushrooms with balsamic reduction

Ingredients:
- 4 portobello mushrooms
- 1/4 cup balsamic vinegar
- 2 tablespoons olive oil
- Salt and pepper to taste

Equipment:
1. Grill pan
2. Tongs
3. Basting brush
4. Saucepan
5. Whisk

Methods:
Step 1: Preheat grill to medium-high heat.

Step 2: Clean the portobello mushrooms and remove stems.

Step 3: Brush mushrooms with olive oil and season with salt and pepper.

Step 4: Place mushrooms on the grill and cook for 4-5 minutes on each side, or until tender.

Step 5: While mushrooms are grilling, prepare the balsamic reduction by simmering balsamic vinegar in a saucepan over medium heat until it thickens.

Step 6: Drizzle balsamic reduction over the grilled portobello mushrooms before serving.

Step 7: Enjoy your delicious grilled portobello mushrooms with balsamic reduction!

Helpful Tips:
1. Clean the portobello mushrooms thoroughly by brushing off any dirt and removing the stems.

2. Marinate the mushrooms in a mixture of olive oil, balsamic vinegar, garlic, salt, and pepper for at least 30 minutes.

3. Preheat your grill to medium-high heat before placing the mushrooms on it.

4. Grill the mushrooms for about 5-7 minutes on each side, or until they are tender and browned.

5. While the mushrooms are grilling, prepare the balsamic reduction by simmering balsamic vinegar and sugar in a saucepan until it thickens.

6. Serve the grilled mushrooms drizzled with the balsamic reduction and enjoy!

Shrimp ceviche with avocado

Ingredients:

- 1 lb shrimp
- 2 avocados
- 2 tomatoes
- 1 red onion
- 1 bunch cilantro
- 3 limes
- Salt and pepper

Equipment:

1. Knife
2. Cutting board
3. Mixing bowl
4. Citrus juicer
5. Spoon
6. Serving platter

Methods:

Step 1: Peel and devein 1 pound of shrimp, then chop into bite-sized pieces.

Step 2: In a large bowl, combine the shrimp with the juice of 4 limes and 2 lemons.

Step 3: Let the shrimp marinate in the citrus juices for about 15 minutes.

Step 4: Dice 1 ripe avocado and add to the shrimp mixture.

Step 5: Stir in 1 diced tomato, 1 diced red onion, 1 diced cucumber, and a handful of chopped cilantro.

Step 6: Season with salt, pepper, and a pinch of red pepper flakes.

Step 7: Cover and refrigerate for at least 30 minutes before serving.

Step 8: Serve the shrimp ceviche with avocado with tortilla chips or on a bed of lettuce. Enjoy!

Helpful Tips:

1. Start by marinating the shrimp in lime juice for at least 30 minutes to "cook" them.

2. Dice ripe avocados and mix them with chopped red onions, diced tomatoes, and chopped cilantro.

3. Add the marinated shrimp to the avocado mixture along with a bit of extra lime juice.

4. Season with salt, pepper, and a pinch of cayenne for a little kick.

5. Let the flavors meld together in the refrigerator for at least 1 hour before serving.

6. Serve the shrimp ceviche with avocado in a bowl with tortilla chips or on a tostada for a delicious and refreshing appetizer or light meal.

Roasted brussels sprouts with garlic and lemon

Ingredients:

- 1 lb brussels sprouts
- 2 cloves garlic, minced
- 1 lemon, juiced
- 2 tbsp olive oil
- Salt and pepper to taste

Equipment:

1. Baking sheet
2. Mixing bowl
3. Knife
4. Cutting board
5. Garlic press
6. Lemon juicer

Methods:

Step 1: Preheat the oven to 400°F.

Step 2: Trim and halve Brussels sprouts, removing any outer leaves that are brown or wilted.

Step 3: Toss Brussels sprouts with olive oil, minced garlic, salt, and pepper in a bowl.

Step 4: Spread Brussels sprouts in a single layer on a baking sheet.

Step 5: Roast in the oven for 25-30 minutes, until tender and caramelized.

Step 6: Remove from the oven and squeeze fresh lemon juice over the Brussels sprouts.

Step 7: Toss to combine and serve hot. Enjoy your delicious roasted Brussels sprouts with garlic and lemon!

Helpful Tips:

1. Preheat your oven to 400°F.

2. Trim and halve the Brussels sprouts, then toss them in olive oil, minced garlic, lemon juice, salt, and pepper.

3. Spread the Brussels sprouts in a single layer on a baking sheet.

4. Roast in the oven for 25-30 minutes, or until they are tender and crispy on the edges.

5. Shake the pan or stir the Brussels sprouts halfway through cooking to ensure even browning.

6. Squeeze additional lemon juice over the roasted Brussels sprouts before serving for a burst of freshness.

7. Optional: sprinkle with Parmesan cheese or toasted pine nuts for extra flavor and texture.

Grilled chicken kabobs with peppers and onions

Ingredients:
- 1 lb chicken breast, cubed
- 1 red bell pepper, cut into chunks
- 1 yellow bell pepper, cut into chunks
- 1 onion, cut into chunks

Equipment:
1. Grill
2. Skewers
3. Tongs
4. Cutting board
5. Knife

Methods:
Step 1: Start by soaking wooden skewers in water for at least 30 minutes to prevent them from burning.

Step 2: Preheat the grill to medium-high heat.

Step 3: Cut boneless, skinless chicken breasts into bite-sized pieces and season with salt, pepper, and your favorite spices.

Step 4: Thread the chicken pieces onto the skewers, alternating with chunks of bell peppers and onions.

Step 5: Brush the kabobs with olive oil and place them on the grill.

Step 6: Grill for 10-12 minutes, turning occasionally, until the chicken is cooked through and the vegetables are tender.

Step 7: Serve the kabobs hot off the grill and enjoy!

Helpful Tips:
1. Marinate the chicken in a mixture of olive oil, lemon juice, garlic, and herbs for at least 30 minutes before grilling.

2. Soak wooden skewers in water for at least 30 minutes before threading with chicken, peppers, and onions to prevent burning.

3. Preheat the grill to medium-high heat and oil the grates to prevent sticking.

4. Cook the kabobs for 10-12 minutes, turning occasionally, until the chicken is cooked through and the vegetables are slightly charred.

5. Serve the kabobs with a side of rice or a salad for a complete meal. Enjoy!

Baked lemon herb cod with green beans

Ingredients:
- 4 cod fillets
- 1 lemon
- 1 tbsp olive oil
- 2 tsp dried oregano
- 1 tsp garlic powder
- 1 lb green beans

Equipment:
1. Baking sheet
2. Mixing bowl
3. Tongs
4. Knife
5. Cutting board

Methods:
Step 1: Preheat oven to 375°F and line a baking sheet with parchment paper.

Step 2: Place cod fillets on the prepared baking sheet.

Step 3: In a small bowl, mix together olive oil, lemon juice, minced garlic, and chopped herbs (such as parsley, dill, and thyme).

Step 4: Brush the herb mixture over the cod fillets.

Step 5: Arrange green beans around the cod on the baking sheet.

Step 6: Drizzle green beans with olive oil, salt, and pepper.

Step 7: Bake in the preheated oven for 15-20 minutes, or until the cod is cooked through and flakes easily with a fork.

Step 8: Serve hot and enjoy!

Helpful Tips:
1. Preheat the oven to 400°F.

2. Season the cod fillets with salt, pepper, lemon juice, herbs (such as thyme or dill), and a drizzle of olive oil.

3. Place the seasoned cod fillets on a baking sheet lined with parchment paper.

4. Arrange fresh green beans around the fillets and drizzle them with olive oil.

5. Bake in the preheated oven for 15-20 minutes, or until the cod is opaque and flakes easily with a fork.

6. Serve the baked lemon herb cod with the roasted green beans for a healthy and delicious meal. Enjoy!

Grilled shrimp salad with citrus dressing

Ingredients:

- 1 lb shrimp
- 8 cups mixed greens
- 2 oranges
- 1/4 cup olive oil
- 2 tbsp lemon juice
- Salt and pepper

Equipment:

1. Grilling pan
2. Mixing bowl
3. Tongs
4. Whisk
5. Serving platter

Methods:

Step 1: Preheat grill to medium-high heat.

Step 2: In a small bowl, whisk together olive oil, lime juice, orange juice, honey, and salt to make the citrus dressing.

Step 3: Thread shrimp onto skewers and brush with olive oil.

Step 4: Grill shrimp for 2-3 minutes per side, until pink and slightly charred.

Step 5: In a large bowl, toss mixed greens, cherry tomatoes, avocado, and red onion.

Step 6: Drizzle citrus dressing over salad and toss to combine.

Step 7: Divide salad onto plates and top with grilled shrimp skewers.

Step 8: Serve and enjoy your delicious grilled shrimp salad with citrus dressing!

Helpful Tips:

1. Start by marinating the shrimp in a mixture of olive oil, garlic, lemon juice, and herbs for at least 30 minutes.

2. Preheat the grill to medium-high heat and cook the shrimp for 2-3 minutes on each side until pink and opaque.

3. In a bowl, mix together mixed greens, cherry tomatoes, cucumbers, and avocado slices for the salad base.

4. Whisk together a dressing of fresh orange juice, olive oil, Dijon mustard, and honey for a tangy citrus flavor.

5. Toss the salad with the dressing, then top with the grilled shrimp and serve immediately for a delicious and refreshing meal.

Egg white frittata with spinach and mushrooms

Ingredients:

- 8 egg whites
- 1 cup chopped spinach
- 1 cup sliced mushrooms
- Salt and pepper to taste

Equipment:

1. Frying pan
2. Spatula
3. Whisk
4. Mixing bowl
5. Knife
6. Cutting board

Methods:

Step 1: Preheat the oven to 350°F.

Step 2: In a large oven-safe skillet, sauté chopped mushrooms and spinach in olive oil until cooked.

Step 3: In a mixing bowl, whisk together 8 egg whites and a pinch of salt and pepper.

Step 4: Pour the egg mixture over the cooked vegetables in the skillet.

Step 5: Cook on the stovetop for about 5 minutes, or until the edges start to set.

Step 6: Transfer the skillet to the preheated oven and bake for 15-20 minutes, or until the frittata is cooked through.

Step 7: Remove from oven and let cool slightly before slicing and serving. Enjoy!

Helpful Tips:

1. Preheat your oven to 350°F and lightly grease a non-stick oven-safe skillet.

2. Saute chopped mushrooms and spinach in a skillet until tender and set aside.

3. Beat egg whites until fluffy and gently fold in the sauteed mixture.

4. Pour the egg white mixture into the skillet and bake for 20-25 minutes until set.

5. For extra flavor, sprinkle with grated Parmesan cheese before baking.

6. Allow the frittata to cool slightly before slicing and serving.

7. Enjoy this healthy and protein-packed dish for breakfast, brunch, or a light dinner.

Zucchini and tomato bake

Ingredients:

- 2 zucchinis
- 4 tomatoes
- 1 cup breadcrumbs
- 1/2 cup grated parmesan
- 2 cloves garlic
- 1/4 cup olive oil
- Salt and pepper to taste

Equipment:

1. Knife
2. Cutting board
3. Baking dish
4. Spoon
5. Mixing bowl

Methods:

Step 1: Preheat the oven to 375°F.

Step 2: Slice 2 zucchinis and 2 tomatoes into thin rounds.

Step 3: In a baking dish, layer the zucchini and tomato slices, alternating between the two.

Step 4: Sprinkle salt, pepper, and dried herbs like oregano and basil over the vegetables.

Step 5: Drizzle olive oil over the vegetables.

Step 6: Cover the dish with foil and bake for 30 minutes.

Step 7: Remove the foil and sprinkle grated cheese on top.

Step 8: Bake for an additional 10-15 minutes until the cheese is golden brown.

Step 9: Serve hot as a delicious side dish.

Helpful Tips:

1. Preheat your oven to 375°F.
2. Slice zucchinis and tomatoes into uniform thickness for even cooking.

3. Layer the zucchini and tomato slices in a baking dish.

4. Sprinkle with salt, pepper, and your favorite herbs or seasonings.

5. Top with grated Parmesan cheese for a crispy finish.

6. Bake for 25-30 minutes or until the vegetables are tender.

7. For added flavor, drizzle with a balsamic glaze or olive oil before serving.

8. Enjoy this flavorful and healthy dish as a side or main course.

Baked tilapia with herb butter

Ingredients:

- 4 tilapia fillets
- 4 tbsp butter
- 2 cloves garlic, minced
- 2 tbsp fresh herbs (such as parsley, dill, or chives)
- Salt and pepper to taste

Equipment:

1. Baking dish
2. Mixing bowl
3. Whisk
4. Basting brush
5. Spatula

Methods:

Step 1: Preheat the oven to 375°F.

Step 2: In a small bowl, mix together softened butter, minced garlic, chopped parsley, lemon juice, salt, and pepper.

Step 3: Place fresh or thawed tilapia fillets on a baking sheet lined with parchment paper.

Step 4: Spread the herb butter mixture evenly over each fillet.

Step 5: Bake the tilapia in the preheated oven for 15-20 minutes, or until the fish is cooked through and flakes easily with a fork.

Step 6: Remove from the oven and serve hot garnished with additional parsley and lemon wedges.

Step 7: Enjoy your delicious baked tilapia with herb butter!

Helpful Tips:

1. Preheat oven to 400°F.

2. Place tilapia fillets in a greased baking dish.

3. In a small bowl, mix melted butter with chopped herbs of your choice (such as parsley, garlic, and lemon zest).

4. Brush herb butter mixture over the tilapia fillets.

5. Season with salt and pepper.

6. Bake for 12-15 minutes or until fish is flaky and fully cooked.

7. Serve with a squeeze of fresh lemon juice and more herbs for garnish.

8. Enjoy your delicious and healthy baked tilapia with herb butter!

Chicken and vegetable stir fry with soy sauce

Ingredients:

- 500g chicken breast
- 1 red bell pepper
- 1 yellow bell pepper
- 1 cup snap peas
- 1/4 cup soy sauce
- 2 tbsp vegetable oil
- 2 cloves garlic

Equipment:

1. Wok
2. Wooden spatula
3. Chef's knife
4. Cutting board
5. Tongs

Methods:

Step 1: Heat oil in a large skillet or wok over medium-high heat.

Step 2: Add diced chicken breast and cook until no longer pink.

Step 3: Add chopped vegetables such as bell peppers, broccoli, carrots, and snow peas to the skillet.

Step 4: Stir frequently and cook until vegetables are tender-crisp.

Step 5: In a small bowl, mix together soy sauce, minced garlic, ginger, and a pinch of sugar.

Step 6: Pour the sauce over the chicken and vegetables in the skillet.

Step 7: Continue to stir and cook for an additional 2-3 minutes.

Step 8: Serve hot over cooked rice. Enjoy your delicious Chicken and Vegetable Stir Fry with Soy Sauce!

Helpful Tips:

1. Start by marinating the chicken in a mixture of soy sauce, garlic, and ginger for at least 30 minutes to infuse flavor.

2. Use a high heat and a large skillet to quickly cook the chicken, allowing it to brown on all sides for a nice sear.

3. Stir-fry your vegetables separately to ensure they are cooked evenly and maintain their crisp texture.

4. Add your marinated chicken back into the skillet with the vegetables and toss everything together with soy sauce until heated through.

5. Serve your chicken and vegetable stir fry over steamed rice or noodles for a complete and satisfying meal.

Quinoa and black bean salad

Ingredients:

- 1 cup quinoa
- 1 can black beans
- 1 red bell pepper
- 1/2 red onion
- 1/4 cup cilantro
- 1 lime
- 2 tbsp olive oil
- Salt and pepper to taste

Equipment:

1. Knife
2. Cutting board
3. Mixing bowl
4. Wooden spoon
5. Skillet

Methods:

Step 1: Rinse 1 cup of quinoa thoroughly in a fine mesh strainer.

Step 2: In a medium saucepan, combine the quinoa with 2 cups of water and bring to a boil.

Step 3: Reduce heat to low, cover, and simmer for about 15 minutes, or until quinoa is cooked and water is absorbed.

Step 4: In a large bowl, combine the cooked quinoa with 1 can of drained and rinsed black beans.

Step 5: Add 1 diced red bell pepper, 1 diced cucumber, 1/4 cup of chopped cilantro, and a squeeze of lime juice.

Step 6: Toss everything together and season with salt and pepper to taste. Enjoy!

Helpful Tips:

1. Rinse the quinoa thoroughly before cooking to remove its natural coating which can taste bitter.

2. Use a ratio of 1 cup quinoa to 2 cups water for cooking.

3. Cook the quinoa according to package instructions, usually simmering for 15-20 minutes until all the water is absorbed.

4. Allow the cooked quinoa to cool before mixing it with the other salad ingredients.

5. Drain and rinse the black beans to remove excess sodium and starch.

6. Add a variety of fresh vegetables like bell peppers, cherry tomatoes, and cucumbers for flavor and crunch.

7. Finish the salad with a simple dressing of olive oil, lemon juice, salt, and pepper.

Grilled swordfish with lemon caper sauce

Ingredients:

- 4 swordfish fillets
- 1/4 cup olive oil
- 2 lemons, juiced
- 2 tbsp capers
- Salt and pepper, to taste
- Fresh parsley, for garnish

Equipment:

1. Grill pan
2. Tongs
3. Spatula
4. Lemon squeezer
5. Whisk

Methods:

Step 1: Preheat the grill to medium-high heat.

Step 2: Season the swordfish steaks with salt, pepper, and a drizzle of olive oil.

Step 3: Grill the swordfish steaks for 4-5 minutes per side, or until they are cooked through.

Step 4: While the swordfish is cooking, make the lemon caper sauce by melting butter in a saucepan and adding capers, lemon juice, and a pinch of salt.

Step 5: Cook the sauce for 2-3 minutes, or until heated through.

Step 6: Serve the grilled swordfish steaks with a drizzle of the lemon caper sauce on top. Enjoy!

Helpful Tips:

1. Season the swordfish with salt, pepper, and olive oil before grilling to enhance the flavors.

2. Preheat your grill to medium-high heat to ensure a proper sear on the swordfish.

3. Cook the swordfish for about 4-5 minutes per side, or until the fish is opaque and flakes easily with a fork.

4. For the lemon caper sauce, sauté minced garlic in butter until fragrant, then add lemon juice and capers.

5. Serve the grilled swordfish with the lemon caper sauce drizzled on top for a burst of flavor. Enjoy!

Baked salmon with dill sauce

Ingredients:
- 4 salmon fillets
- 1/4 cup chopped fresh dill
- 1/4 cup Greek yogurt
- 2 cloves minced garlic
- Salt and pepper to taste
- 1 lemon, sliced

Equipment:
1. Baking dish
2. Mixing bowl
3. Whisk
4. Saucepan
5. Serving platter

Methods:
Step 1: Preheat oven to 375°F.

Step 2: Place salmon fillets on a baking sheet lined with parchment paper.

Step 3: Season salmon with salt, pepper, and a drizzle of olive oil.

Step 4: Bake salmon in the preheated oven for 12-15 minutes, or until the internal temperature reaches 145°F.

Step 5: Meanwhile, prepare the dill sauce by combining mayonnaise, sour cream, dill, lemon juice, salt, and pepper in a bowl.

Step 6: Serve the baked salmon with the dill sauce drizzled on top.

Step 7: Garnish with additional fresh dill if desired. Enjoy your baked salmon with dill sauce!

Helpful Tips:
1. Preheat oven to 400°F and line a baking sheet with foil.

2. Place salmon fillets on the baking sheet and season with salt, pepper, and a squeeze of lemon juice.

3. Bake in the preheated oven for 12-15 minutes, or until the salmon flakes easily with a fork.

4. In a small bowl, mix together yogurt, chopped dill, lemon juice, salt, and pepper to make the dill sauce.

5. Serve the baked salmon with the dill sauce drizzled on top and garnish with extra fresh dill. Enjoy with a side of roasted vegetables or rice.

Shrimp and avocado salad with lime dressing

Ingredients:
- 1 lb shrimp
- 2 ripe avocados
- 4 cups mixed greens
- 1/4 cup olive oil
- 2 limes (juiced)
- Salt and pepper to taste

Equipment:
1. Knife
2. Cutting board
3. Mixing bowl
4. Whisk
5. Salad spinner
6. Serving spoon

Methods:
Step 1: Begin by heating a grill or grill pan over medium heat.

Step 2: In a small bowl, whisk together 1/4 cup of olive oil, the juice of 2 limes, 1 teaspoon of honey, 1 clove of minced garlic, salt, and pepper to make the lime dressing.

Step 3: Peel and devein 1 pound of shrimp, then toss them in a bowl with olive oil, salt, and pepper.

Step 4: Grill the shrimp for 2-3 minutes on each side until they are pink and cooked through.

Step 5: In a large bowl, combine diced avocado, cherry tomatoes, red onion, and the grilled shrimp.

Step 6: Drizzle the lime dressing over the salad and toss to coat.

Step 7: Serve the shrimp and avocado salad with lime dressing immediately and enjoy!

Helpful Tips:

1. Start by marinating your shrimp in lime juice, garlic, and chili flakes for extra flavor.

2. Cook the shrimp until pink and opaque, being careful not to overcook.

3. Cube your avocado and toss it with fresh lime juice to prevent browning.

4. Combine the shrimp and avocado in a bowl with cherry tomatoes, red onion, and cilantro.

5. Drizzle with a dressing made from lime juice, olive oil, honey, and salt and pepper.

6. Mix everything together gently to avoid mushing the avocado.

7. Serve your shrimp and avocado salad chilled for a refreshing summer dish.

Roasted sweet potatoes with herbs

Ingredients:

- 2 large sweet potatoes
- 2 tbsp olive oil
- 1 tsp dried rosemary
- 1 tsp dried thyme
- Salt and pepper to taste

Equipment:

1. Baking sheet
2. Mixing bowl
3. Tongs
4. Chef's knife
5. Cutting board

Methods:

Step 1: Preheat your oven to 400°F

Step 2: Wash and peel 2 pounds of sweet potatoes

Step 3: Cut the sweet potatoes into 1-inch cubes

Step 4: In a large bowl, toss the sweet potatoes with 2 tablespoons of olive oil, 1 teaspoon of salt, 1 teaspoon of pepper, and 1 tablespoon of chopped fresh herbs (such as rosemary or thyme)

Step 5: Spread the sweet potatoes in a single layer on a baking sheet

Step 6: Roast in the oven for 30-35 minutes, or until the sweet potatoes are tender and starting to brown

Step 7: Serve hot and enjoy!

Helpful Tips:

1. Preheat your oven to 400°F.

2. Peel and chop sweet potatoes into bite-sized pieces.

3. Toss sweet potatoes with olive oil, salt, pepper, and your favorite dried herbs (such as rosemary, thyme, or sage).

4. Spread the sweet potatoes in a single layer on a baking sheet.

5. Roast for 25-30 minutes, flipping halfway through, until they are tender and slightly crispy.

6. Serve hot as a delicious side dish or snack.

7. Don't overcrowd the baking sheet to ensure even cooking.

8. Experiment with different herb combinations to customize the flavor to your liking. Enjoy!

Turkey and vegetable skillet

Ingredients:

- 1 lb ground turkey
- 1 bell pepper, diced
- 1 zucchini, sliced
- 1 onion, chopped
- 1 tsp garlic powder
- 1 tsp onion powder
- Salt and pepper to taste

Equipment:

1. Skillet
2. Wooden spoon
3. Tongs
4. Knife
5. Cutting board

Methods:

Step 1: Heat olive oil in a large skillet over medium heat.

Step 2: Add diced onion and minced garlic, sauté until fragrant.

Step 3: Add diced turkey breast, cook until browned.

Step 4: Stir in chopped bell pepper, zucchini, and cherry tomatoes.

Step 5: Season with salt, pepper, and Italian seasoning.

Step 6: Cook until vegetables are tender and turkey is cooked through.

Step 7: Serve hot with a sprinkle of fresh parsley on top.

Step 8: Enjoy your delicious and nutritious Turkey and vegetable skillet!

Helpful Tips:

1. Start by preparing your ingredients: dice the turkey and chop the vegetables into bite-sized pieces.

2. Heat a large skillet over medium heat and add oil.

3. Cook the turkey until browned and cooked through, then remove from skillet.

4. Add more oil to the skillet and sauté the vegetables until slightly tender.

5. Season with your favorite herbs and spices, like garlic, thyme, or rosemary.

6. Add the cooked turkey back to the skillet and mix everything together.

7. Let it simmer for a few minutes to let the flavors meld together.

8. Serve hot and enjoy your delicious turkey and vegetable skillet!

Cauliflower crust pizza with vegetables

Ingredients:

- 1 head cauliflower
- 1/2 cup shredded mozzarella
- 1/4 cup grated Parmesan
- 1/2 tsp dried oregano
- 1/2 tsp garlic powder
- 1/4 tsp salt
- 1/4 tsp black pepper
- 1/4 cup marinara sauce
- 1/2 cup assorted vegetables

Equipment:

1. Baking sheet
2. Pizza cutter
3. Cutting board
4. Chef's knife
5. Skillet

Methods:

Step 1: Preheat the oven to 425°F.

Step 2: Cut a head of cauliflower into florets and pulse in a food processor until it resembles rice.

Step 3: Microwave the cauliflower rice for 5 minutes, then squeeze out excess moisture with a kitchen towel.

Step 4: Mix the cauliflower rice with 1 beaten egg, 1/2 cup shredded mozzarella, 1 teaspoon dried oregano, and salt and pepper.

Step 5: Press the mixture onto a baking sheet lined with parchment paper to form a crust.

Step 6: Bake the crust for 15-20 minutes until golden brown.

Step 7: Top with tomato sauce, veggies, and cheese, then bake for an additional 10-15 minutes. Enjoy your delicious cauliflower crust pizza with vegetables!

Helpful Tips:

1. Preheat your oven to 425°F.

2. Pulse cauliflower florets in a food processor until they resemble rice, then cook in a skillet until tender.

3. Squeeze out excess moisture from the cooked cauliflower using a kitchen towel.

4. Mix cauliflower with cheese, egg, and seasonings to create the crust.

5. Spread the mixture onto a lined baking sheet and shape into a round crust.

6. Bake for 15-20 minutes until golden brown.

7. Top with your favorite vegetables and cheese, then bake again until cheese is melted.

8. Enjoy your delicious and nutritious cauliflower crust pizza!

Grilled chicken thighs with roasted broccoli

Ingredients:
- 8 chicken thighs
- 1 head of broccoli
- 2 tbsp olive oil
- Salt and pepper to taste

Equipment:
1. Grill pan
2. Baking sheet
3. Tongs
4. Knife
5. Cutting board

Methods:
Step 1: Preheat the grill to medium-high heat.

Step 2: Season the chicken thighs with salt, pepper, and your favorite spices.

Step 3: Place the chicken thighs on the grill and cook for 6-8 minutes per side, or until the internal temperature reaches 165°F.

Step 4: Toss the broccoli florets with olive oil, salt, and pepper.

Step 5: Spread the broccoli out on a baking sheet and roast in a preheated oven at 400°F for 20-25 minutes, or until tender and slightly crispy.

Step 6: Serve the grilled chicken thighs with the roasted broccoli on the side. Enjoy your delicious and healthy meal!

Helpful Tips:
1. Preheat your grill to medium-high heat.

2. Season the chicken thighs with salt, pepper, and your favorite herbs or spices.

3. Grill the chicken thighs for about 6-8 minutes on each side, or until they reach an internal temperature of 165°F.

4. Toss broccoli florets with olive oil, salt, and pepper.

5. Roast the broccoli in a preheated oven at 400°F for about 20-25 minutes, flipping halfway through.

6. Serve the grilled chicken thighs and roasted broccoli together for a delicious and healthy meal.

Lentil and vegetable stir fry

Ingredients:

- 1 cup red lentils
- 2 cups mixed vegetables
- 1 onion, diced
- 2 cloves garlic, minced
- 1 tsp cumin
- 1 tsp coriander
- 1/2 tsp turmeric
- Salt and pepper to taste

Equipment:

1. Skillet
2. Wooden spoon
3. Chef's knife
4. Cutting board
5. Tongs

Methods:

Step 1: Rinse 1 cup of lentils and cook them according to package instructions.

Step 2: Chop up an assortment of your favorite vegetables like bell peppers, broccoli, and carrots.

Step 3: Heat a large skillet over medium heat and add 1 tablespoon of oil.

Step 4: Add the chopped vegetables to the skillet and stir fry for 5-7 minutes until they start to soften.

Step 5: Season with salt, pepper, and any other desired seasonings.

Step 6: Add the cooked lentils to the skillet and mix well with the vegetables.

Step 7: Cook for another 2-3 minutes, then serve hot. Enjoy your Lentil and Vegetable Stir Fry!

Helpful Tips:

1. Start by rinsing the lentils thoroughly to remove any debris or dirt.

2. Chop up a variety of colorful vegetables such as bell peppers, carrots, and broccoli for added flavor and nutrients.

3. Heat a large skillet or wok over medium-high heat and add a bit of oil.

4. Stir in the lentils and vegetables, cooking until they are tender but still slightly crisp.

5. Season with salt, pepper, and your favorite herbs or spices for added flavor.

6. Serve the stir fry on its own or over a bed of rice or quinoa for a complete meal.

Baked trout with lemon herb butter

Ingredients:

- 4 whole trout
- 1/2 cup butter
- 2 lemons
- 1 tsp minced garlic
- 1 tbsp chopped parsley
- Salt and pepper to taste

Equipment:

1. Baking dish
2. Mixing bowl
3. Whisk
4. Knife
5. Cutting board

Methods:

Step 1: Preheat the oven to 400°F and line a baking sheet with aluminum foil.

Step 2: Rinse the trout under cold water and pat dry with paper towels.

Step 3: Season the trout with salt and pepper, both inside and out.

Step 4: In a small bowl, mix together melted butter, minced garlic, chopped fresh herbs (such as parsley, dill, and thyme), and lemon juice.

Step 5: Stuff the herb butter mixture inside the trout cavity.

Step 6: Place the trout on the prepared baking sheet and bake for 15-20 minutes, until the flesh is opaque and flaky.

Step 7: Serve the baked trout with additional lemon wedges and enjoy!

Helpful Tips:

1. Preheat your oven to 375°F.
2. Rinse and pat dry the trout fillets.
3. Mix softened butter with lemon juice, garlic, and chopped herbs.
4. Season both sides of the trout with salt and pepper.
5. Place the trout fillets on a baking dish lined with foil.

6. Spread the lemon herb butter mixture over the fillets.

7. Bake for 15-20 minutes or until the trout is cooked through.

8. Garnish with fresh herbs and lemon slices before serving.

9. Serve with a side of roasted vegetables or a light salad.

10. Enjoy your delicious and healthy meal!

Shrimp and vegetable stir fry with ginger

Ingredients:
- 1 pound of shrimp
- 2 tablespoons of soy sauce
- 1 tablespoon of sesame oil
- 1/2 teaspoon of ground ginger
- 1 bell pepper, sliced
- 1 onion, sliced
- 2 cloves of garlic
- 1 tablespoon of vegetable oil

Equipment:
1. Wok
2. Wooden spatula
3. Chef's knife
4. Cutting board
5. Paring knife

Methods:

Step 1: Heat a tablespoon of oil in a large skillet or wok over high heat.

Step 2: Add 1 pound of peeled and deveined shrimp to the skillet and cook until pink and opaque, about 2-3 minutes per side.

Step 3: Remove the shrimp from the skillet and set aside.

Step 4: Add 2 cloves of minced garlic and a tablespoon of grated ginger to the skillet and cook for 1 minute.

Step 5: Add 2 cups of sliced bell peppers, 1 cup of sliced carrots, and 1 cup of snap peas to the skillet and cook until tender-crisp, about 5 minutes.

Step 6: Add the shrimp back to the skillet and toss everything together.

Step 7: Serve the shrimp and vegetable stir fry with ginger over cooked rice or noodles. Enjoy!

Helpful Tips:

1. Start by marinating the shrimp in a mixture of soy sauce, ginger, garlic, and sesame oil for at least 30 minutes for maximum flavor.

2. Prepare your vegetables (bell peppers, broccoli, snap peas, etc.) by cutting them into evenly sized pieces for even cooking.

3. Heat a wok or large skillet over high heat with a small amount of oil.

4. Stir fry the shrimp until pink and opaque, then remove from the pan.

5. Add more oil to the pan and stir fry the vegetables until they are slightly tender but still crisp.

6. Return the shrimp to the pan, toss everything together and serve hot over rice or noodles. Enjoy!

Egg white and spinach breakfast burrito

Ingredients:
- 8 egg whites
- 1 cup spinach
- 1/4 cup diced tomatoes
- 1/4 cup shredded cheese

Equipment:
1. Skillet
2. Mixing bowl
3. Whisk
4. Spatula
5. Cutting board
6. Knife

Methods:
Step 1: Heat a non-stick skillet over medium heat.

Step 2: In a small bowl, whisk together 4 egg whites with salt and pepper.

Step 3: Pour the egg mixture into the skillet and let it cook for 1-2 minutes, stirring occasionally.

Step 4: Add a handful of spinach to the eggs and continue cooking until the spinach wilts.

Step 5: Spoon the egg mixture onto a whole wheat tortilla.

Step 6: Top with salsa or hot sauce if desired.

Step 7: Roll up the tortilla, tucking in the sides as you go.

Step 8: Enjoy your delicious and healthy breakfast burrito!

Helpful Tips:
1. Whisk the egg whites until frothy to make them light and fluffy.

2. Sauté the spinach with garlic and olive oil for extra flavor.

3. Season the egg whites and spinach with salt, pepper, and any preferred herbs or spices.

4. Add a sprinkle of cheese for added creaminess and flavor, if desired.

5. Warm the tortilla before assembling the burrito to make it easier to wrap.

6. Roll the burrito tightly to prevent it from falling apart while eating.

7. Serve with salsa or avocado for a delicious and nutritious breakfast option.

Baked eggplant Parmesan with marinara sauce

Ingredients:
- 1 large eggplant
- 1 cup marinara sauce
- 1 cup breadcrumbs
- 1 cup grated Parmesan cheese
- 2 eggs, beaten
- Salt and pepper to taste

Equipment:
1. Baking dish
2. Mixing bowl
3. Whisk
4. Spatula
5. Grater
6. Knife

Methods:
Step 1: Preheat oven to 400°F and grease a baking dish with olive oil.

Step 2: Slice an eggplant into 1/4-inch rounds and sprinkle with salt. Let sit for 15 minutes, then rinse and pat dry.

Step 3: Dip eggplant slices in beaten egg, then coat in a mixture of breadcrumbs, Parmesan cheese, and Italian seasoning.

Step 4: Place coated eggplant slices in a single layer in the baking dish.

Step 5: Top eggplant slices with marinara sauce and shredded mozzarella cheese.

Step 6: Bake in the oven for 25-30 minutes, or until cheese is melted and bubbly.

Step 7: Serve hot and enjoy!

Helpful Tips:
1. Preheat your oven to 375°F.

2. Slice the eggplant into 1/4 inch rounds and sprinkle with salt to help draw out excess moisture.

3. After 15 minutes, rinse the eggplant slices and pat dry with a paper towel.

4. Dip each slice into beaten egg, then coat with breadcrumbs and grated Parmesan cheese.

5. Arrange the slices on a baking sheet and bake for 20 minutes, or until golden brown.

6. In a separate saucepan, heat marinara sauce until warm.

7. Layer the baked eggplant slices in a casserole dish with marinara sauce and mozzarella cheese.

8. Bake for an additional 10-15 minutes, or until the cheese is melted and bubbly. Enjoy!

Grilled portobello mushrooms with garlic and herbs

Ingredients:

- 4 portobello mushrooms
- 4 cloves of garlic
- 1 tbsp olive oil
- 1 tsp dried herbs

Equipment:

1. Grill
2. Knife
3. Cutting board
4. Tongs
5. Mixing bowl

Methods:

Step 1: Clean the portobello mushrooms by wiping them with a damp paper towel to remove any dirt.

Step 2: Remove the stems from the mushrooms and place them in a shallow dish.

Step 3: In a small bowl, mix together minced garlic, olive oil, chopped herbs (such as thyme, rosemary, and parsley), salt, and pepper.

Step 4: Pour the garlic and herb mixture over the mushrooms, making sure they are well coated.

Step 5: Preheat a grill or grill pan over medium heat.

Step 6: Place the mushrooms on the grill and cook for about 4-5 minutes on each side, until they are tender.

Step 7: Serve the grilled portobello mushrooms hot as a side dish or on top of a salad. Enjoy!

Helpful Tips:

1. Clean the portobello mushrooms by wiping them with a damp paper towel to remove any dirt.

2. Remove the stems from the mushrooms and scrape out the gills with a spoon to prevent them from becoming watery.

3. Marinate the mushrooms in a mixture of minced garlic, your favorite herbs (such as thyme, rosemary, or parsley), olive oil, salt, and pepper for at least 30 minutes.

4. Preheat your grill to medium-high heat and place the mushrooms directly on the grates, gill-side up.

5. Cook for 4-5 minutes on each side until they are tender and evenly charred.

6. Serve the grilled portobello mushrooms as a side dish or atop a salad or sandwich for a delicious and flavorful meal. Enjoy!

Turkey meatball lettuce wraps

Ingredients:
- 1 lb ground turkey
- 2 cloves garlic, minced
- 1 tsp cumin
- 1 tsp paprika
- Salt and pepper
- 8 leaves lettuce

Equipment:
1. Mixing bowl
2. Skillet
3. Tongs
4. Cutting board
5. Knife

Methods:
Step 1: Preheat oven to 400°F and line a baking sheet with parchment paper.

Step 2: In a large bowl, combine ground turkey, breadcrumbs, minced garlic, chopped parsley, salt, pepper, and egg.

Step 3: Form mixture into small meatballs and place on the prepared baking sheet.

Step 4: Bake meatballs for 15-20 minutes or until cooked through.

Step 5: In the meantime, wash and dry lettuce leaves and prepare desired toppings such as diced tomatoes, shredded carrots, and sliced cucumbers.

Step 6: Once meatballs are cooked, assemble lettuce wraps by placing meatballs in lettuce leaves and adding toppings.

Step 7: Enjoy your turkey meatball lettuce wraps!

Helpful Tips:
1. Use lean ground turkey to keep the meatballs juicy and flavorful.

2. Add diced onions, garlic, and fresh herbs like parsley or cilantro for extra flavor.

3. Form meatballs into small, bite-sized portions for easier wrapping in lettuce leaves.

4. Ensure the lettuce leaves are large and sturdy enough to hold the meatballs without tearing.

5. Serve with a tangy and flavorful dipping sauce, like a spicy sriracha mayo or a sweet teriyaki glaze.

6. Garnish with sliced avocado, shredded carrots, and crunchy peanuts for added texture and flavor.

Baked chicken drumsticks with barbecue sauce

Ingredients:

- 8 chicken drumsticks
- 1 cup barbecue sauce
- 1 tbsp olive oil
- Salt and pepper to taste

Equipment:

1. Baking sheet
2. Tongs
3. Brush
4. Knife
5. Cutting board

Methods:

Step 1: Preheat the oven to 400°F (200°C).

Step 2: Season the chicken drumsticks with salt, pepper, and any additional desired seasonings.

Step 3: Place the seasoned chicken drumsticks on a baking sheet lined with aluminum foil.

Step 4: Bake the chicken drumsticks in the preheated oven for 25-30 minutes.

Step 5: Remove the chicken drumsticks from the oven and brush them with barbecue sauce.

Step 6: Return the chicken drumsticks to the oven and bake for an additional 10-15 minutes, or until cooked through.

Step 7: Remove the chicken drumsticks from the oven and let them rest for a few minutes before serving. Enjoy!

Helpful Tips:

1. Preheat your oven to 400°F.
2. Season the chicken drumsticks with salt, pepper, and your favorite spices.
3. Place the drumsticks on a baking sheet lined with foil for easy cleanup.

4. Bake for 25-30 minutes, or until the internal temperature reaches 165°F.

5. Brush the drumsticks with barbecue sauce during the last 10 minutes of cooking.

6. For extra flavor, marinate the drumsticks in the barbecue sauce for at least 30 minutes before cooking.

7. Serve with your favorite side dishes like coleslaw, corn on the cob, or baked beans.

8. Enjoy your delicious homemade barbecue chicken drumsticks!

Roasted Brussel sprouts with lemon and garlic

Ingredients:

- 1 lb Brussel sprouts
- 2 tbsp olive oil
- 2 cloves garlic, minced
- 1 lemon, juice and zest
- Salt and pepper to taste

Equipment:

1. Baking sheet
2. Paring knife
3. Mixing bowl
4. Wooden spoon
5. Garlic press

Methods:

Step 1: Preheat the oven to 400°F.

Step 2: Wash and dry 1 pound of Brussel sprouts, then trim the ends and cut in half.

Step 3: In a bowl, toss the halved Brussel sprouts with 2 tablespoons of olive oil, the juice of 1 lemon, 2 minced garlic cloves, salt, and pepper.

Step 4: Spread the Brussel sprouts in a single layer on a baking sheet.

Step 5: Roast in the preheated oven for 25-30 minutes, or until browned and crispy.

Step 6: Serve hot, garnished with lemon zest if desired. Enjoy your delicious Roasted Brussel sprouts with lemon and garlic!

Helpful Tips:

1. Preheat your oven to 400°F.

2. Wash and trim the ends of the Brussels sprouts, then cut them in half.

3. Toss the Brussels sprouts with olive oil, minced garlic, lemon juice, salt, and pepper in a mixing bowl.

4. Spread the Brussels sprouts out in a single layer on a baking sheet.

5. Roast in the oven for 25-30 minutes, or until they are tender and lightly browned.

6. Squeeze fresh lemon juice over the top before serving for extra flavor. Enjoy!

Grilled chicken kabobs with bell peppers and onions

Ingredients:
- 1 lb chicken breast
- 1 red bell pepper
- 1 yellow bell pepper
- 1 onion
- 2 tbsp olive oil
- Salt and pepper to taste

Equipment:
1. Grill
2. Skewers
3. Knife
4. Cutting board
5. Tongs
6. Mixing bowl

Methods:
Step 1: Soak wooden skewers in water for at least 30 minutes to prevent them from burning.

Step 2: Preheat grill to medium-high heat.

Step 3: Cut chicken breasts into bite-sized pieces and season with salt, pepper, and your favorite herbs and spices.

Step 4: Cut bell peppers and onions into chunks of similar size to the chicken.

Step 5: Thread chicken, bell peppers, and onions onto skewers, alternating between each ingredient.

Step 6: Brush kabobs with olive oil to prevent sticking.

Step 7: Grill kabobs for 10-15 minutes, turning occasionally, or until chicken is cooked through.

Step 8: Serve hot and enjoy!

Helpful Tips:

1. Soak wooden skewers in water for at least 30 minutes to prevent burning.

2. Cut chicken, bell peppers, and onions into evenly sized pieces for even cooking.

3. Marinate chicken in a mixture of olive oil, lemon juice, garlic, and herbs for at least 30 minutes for added flavor.

4. Preheat grill to medium-high heat and lightly oil the grates to prevent sticking.

5. Thread chicken and vegetables onto skewers, alternating for a colorful presentation.

6. Grill kabobs for 10-12 minutes, turning occasionally, until chicken is cooked through and vegetables are tender.

7. Serve hot with a side of rice or salad for a complete meal. Bon appétit!

Baked lemon herb cod with steamed green beans.

Ingredients:

- 1 lb cod fillets
- 1 lemon
- 1 tbsp olive oil
- 1 tsp dried herbs
- 1 lb green beans

Equipment:

1. Baking dish
2. Tongs
3. Spatula
4. Steamer basket
5. Frying pan

Methods:

Step 1: Preheat the oven to 400°F.

Step 2: Season cod fillets with salt, pepper, lemon zest, and chopped herbs.

Step 3: Place the seasoned cod fillets on a baking sheet lined with parchment paper.

Step 4: Drizzle olive oil over the cod fillets.

Step 5: Bake the cod fillets in the preheated oven for 15-20 minutes, or until cooked through.

Step 6: While the cod is baking, steam the green beans until tender-crisp.

Step 7: Season the green beans with salt, pepper, and a squeeze of lemon juice.

Step 8: Serve the baked lemon herb cod with the steamed green beans. Enjoy your meal!

Helpful Tips:

1. Preheat your oven to 400°F before you start cooking.

2. Season your cod fillets with salt, pepper, and a generous amount of lemon juice and fresh herbs like parsley or dill.

3. Place the seasoned cod fillets on a baking tray lined with parchment paper.

4. Bake the cod in the preheated oven for 15-20 minutes or until it flakes easily with a fork.

5. While the cod is baking, steam your green beans until they are tender-crisp.

6. Serve the baked lemon herb cod with the steamed green beans on the side for a healthy and delicious meal.

Milton Keynes UK
Ingram Content Group UK Ltd.
UKHW020738010424
440421UK00014B/870